Finding Sherri

Reclaiming Myself after Childhood Sexual Assault

Sherri Noble Jones

and

Amy Cherie Copeland

Hidden
Owl, LLC

Edited by Amy Cherie Copeland
Cover and layout by Richard Levine

Sherri Noble Jones wrote her story.
Amy Cherie Copeland wrote the "Did you know?" sections.

WUASM logo on the back cover used with the permission of Women United Against Sexual Molestation.

All photos are the property of Sherri Noble Jones except for the following:
"Off to School," used with the permission of Spokane Public Schools, Spokane, Washington.
"The Green Shanty Shack," attributed to Image Capture: May 2023 © 2023 Google.
Photo of Amy Cherie Copeland used with the permission of Olivia Onate.

ISBN: 979-8-9867824-1-6

www.wuasm.org

Published by Hidden Owl, LLC
Hiddenowl.com

This memoir depicts actual events in the life of the author and reflects the author's present recollections of experiences over time. Some events have been compressed, and some dialogue has been recreated. While all persons within are actual individuals, names and identifying characteristics of some people have been changed to respect their privacy.

Advance praise for *Finding Sherri: Reclaiming Myself after Childhood Sexual Assault*

"Honest and tender, Sherri does a beautiful job packing an entire lifetime into a well told digestible morsel. Not just a story, this book includes tidbits of psychoeducation about the long-term effects of complex trauma, to help readers understand the statistical outcomes for those who have experienced it. Both the story and the education are invaluable, not only to help those with similar stories feel less alone but also to educate everyone on the very real, lasting effects of childhood abuse."

—Brooks Decker, Mental Health Counselor

"In an air of true transparency, Sherri Jones shares her life story with a raw depiction of how childhood trauma impacted her life. Shrouded in secrecy, she kept the pain and accounts of violence to herself, not aware of how these experiences would influence her life choices as an adult. She hopes each reader will be encouraged to examine painful experiences in their lives and empowered to begin a journey to healing, one that will move them to survivors."

—Karen Boone, Founder & CEO
I Am Spokane, A Civic Ambassador Initiative

"First things first: Proceed with caution. This book deals with childhood sexual abuse. This is an extremely powerful story of a young person who survives the unthinkable, not without scars, but the key word here is that she survives. There are multiple individuals whose experiences may have been told before, but rarely with such freshness, intensity, and power. Sherri Jones is an inspiration."

—Millie Sagesse, L.M.H.C.

"This book illuminates the darkness, embarrassment, and shame associated with trauma resulting from sexual abuse. Sherri gives a triumphant account of her lived experiences and brilliantly describes her journey from victim to survivor to overcomer. Through bravely sharing her personal story juxtaposed with the known ramifications of this type of trauma, Sherri provides a source of comfort for the reader in knowing they are not alone. This book has the ability to be a catalyst to propel survivors onto a path of reclaiming their freedom through healing."

—Cara Baker, MN, BSN

"This chilling story told by Sherri Jones depicts the real life of so many women today. She hid the trauma and ran from herself, concealing her inner truths and sworn to secrecy, only to discover she was lost in a life influenced by the pain from her past. This is a must-read for women who were innocent victims from childhood and continue to run from themselves as adults. Sherri's story provides hope and incites women to take their lives back, embrace the beauty from within, love themselves, and be themselves."

—Victoria Kirkpatrick

Table of Contents

Acknowledgments

First, I want to thank God for blessing me to finally assemble my thoughts and put them on paper. My story is true and I have tried not to leave out anything I thought would benefit another precious soul who has gone through life-changing experiences. Without God, we can do nothing!

My parents Everett and Violet Noble are no longer here with me. At the end of her life Mom said to me, "You can do anything you put your mind to." Thank you for all your encouragement in helping me get my non-profit thoughts together. RIH mom (1927-2022).

To my four beautiful children, thank you for all your help in making my dream come true. In 2015 when I was attacked by a guy on Harts Road in Jacksonville, Florida, you convinced me to do something about my life story. There were times when I couldn't write because I thought I couldn't get the right words on paper. But thanks to you, at last my book is getting published. I am forever grateful for the drive for me to complete my book.

To my beautiful grandchildren, may you always be protected as life takes you through many turns. Remember *no* means **no**, so speak up in any situation you may encounter that is wrong. Don't live carrying someone else's wronged baggage.

Karen (Harvey) Boone, thank you for your writing talent that got my story into many newspaper articles. Without your expertise I couldn't have done it alone. I've known Karen since my teenage years, and she has known me through many trials in my life, so she was able to assist in many areas of my non-profit organization, Women United Against Sexual Molestation. With her wisdom, love, and unfailing support, she would take my writing and turn it into the dialogue I was trying to say.

To my editor and co-author Amy Cherie Copeland, wow, in January 2023 when I was introduced to you my writing was a wreck. You showed me how to be more descriptive in writing my sentences. You never judged too harshly but spoke with grace to help me better understand what I needed to improve. Thank you for your time and support. You will always be in my conversations when I speak about my book *Finding Sherri*.

Charles Beyer, Judith Julian, and Olivia Onate were our proofreaders. Many thanks to all three of you for your careful reading to help us make this book the best it could be.

Cleveland Thomas, my fiancée, without your love, inspiration, and education on how to make words sound more professional, I would not be this far. You have given me tips for writing my story as well as the title *Finding Sherri*. May God always bless you!

Finding Sherri

Chapter One: A Spring Morning

1974

What a beautiful way to start my Saturday morning. The sun is peeping through the clouds and shining through my white curtains that have baby birds on them. After a long week at school, the weekend is just getting started. Outside my bedroom window closest to the driveway of my parents' house I hear chirping from the birds in the beautiful brown oak tree that sits next door in my neighbor's yard. The leaves are turning green which means spring is fast approaching. The birds are busy building nests out of pine needles, twigs, grass, hair, and other items they can conjure up. I can see the birds fly down from the tree to the top of our old wooden shed and then off again into the blue sky.

On weekend mornings when I was fourteen, I would watch the birds come and go to the tree. Then I would get dressed, eat breakfast, and go outside and watch them some more. I always knew when the new arrivals hatched because I would hear a different kind of chirp. The baby birds were whining for some food from their mom. I would want to climb the tree to see what was going on but the nests were way too high.

One sunny day when I was outside observing the festivities, I looked on the ground in the driveway and to my surprise, what did I see lying in the dirt? It was a small, gray-black, chirping baby bird that had fallen out of the oak tree. The little bird was injured. The wind was blowing lightly so I assumed that's why he fell from his safe place called home.

I ran into the house to get a shoe box since I had gotten a pair of shoes last week. I grabbed some paper towels and an old white towel to pick up my injured bird, though I was not quite sure how I was going to pick it up, or if it would still be there when I got back. I ran down our cement stairs and the sidewalk to the bumpy dirt driveway. To my surprise the soft little gray-black bird was still there. I scooped it up with the paper towels and placed it in the tiny shoe box.

I examined the baby bird to see where his injuries were since he was not trying to fly. His little eyes looked pitifully at me and I at him. I located what appeared to be a broken neck. I assumed it was broken because his head wouldn't stay up. *Ouch.*

He barely flapped his little wings. I used a popsicle stick and a piece of yarn to prop his neck up. I ran into the house with my bird in the box to my mother who was a nurse, just hoping she had some better news.

Mom looked and said, "His neck is broken and he will probably die."

Although I was sad for the rest of the day, I kept hoping when I woke in the morning the ill bird would still be alive. The next morning I heard the usual bird songs outside my window, but my bird friend in the shoebox was not among the chirping chorus; it was deceased. This was the first time something close to me had passed away. *This whole day is ruined. I thought I had done everything possible to keep him alive.*

I gave the baby bird a perfect burial by wrapping him in more paper towels. Then I made a cross out of sticks and put some rocks around so I would know where he was buried. To get over it, I decided I would design clothes for my Barbie dolls since that is what I generally did on Saturdays.

Mom was my inspiration for Barbie fashion. She was always dressed in the latest fashions and had a striking figure with skin so light my friends believed she was Japanese. On this day, she was packing to go on a trip to Seattle for a women's church meeting for the weekend. When I told her about the bird's demise, Mom comforted me and said, "Things will be OK. You'll get another pet one day soon."

Mom had it hard growing up so she only wanted us to excel in whatever we did. By us, I mean my siblings and me. I had an older brother Robertus who was in the Army. My older sister Gianna was also grown and living independently, so I was the baby bird still in the nest. Mom brought structure and discipline to the household, maintaining a clean and orderly home for us. She may have addressed some issues harshly but that was Mom; we knew she loved us and always encouraged us to do better.

People from the church often visited our home to seek advice from my mom. They knew they could trust her wisdom. I would overhear, "How do I get my husband to open my car door or get things done around the house?"

Mom would reply, "By much prayer and by letting him know what you desire in a nice way." Sometimes I would hear Mom say, "You just have to wait on God" to fix certain things.

Mom was busy preparing her suitcase with packing the last items so Barbie clothes would have to wait. I assisted her by making sure she didn't forget her toothpaste, deodorant, medication, etc. Helping Mom gave me more time to ask her questions. I always had something to ask her.

My dad was outside in his blue overalls detailing mom's white Lincoln Continental, something he was proud to do. Dad always kept her car cleaned, waxed, and detailed inside and out. He worked extra hours as a professional tractor painter to make sure Mom had enough money to travel and shop on her church trips.

When Mom was ready to load the car and leave for Seattle, she said to my dad in her firm voice, "Everett, I'm ready to get on the road." Dad came inside, gathered her luggage, and put it in the trunk.

Before Mom left, we prayed for her safe travels there and back. Then Mom marched her 5'5" frame out to the driveway as if to say, "I'm going somewhere so get out of my way."

On this day as Mom's Lincoln rolled away from our house, I felt especially overwhelmed with emotion. I always teared up when Mom left on her trips, probably because I thought she wasn't coming back. Mom told me I was adopted when I was about six, and although I knew she wasn't my real mom, I didn't understand why my birth mother wasn't around. I didn't know the name of it back then but it's called *separation anxiety.*

Sherri's adoptive parents, Everett and Violet Noble.

Did you <u>know</u>?

Separation anxiety is a common part of development for babies and children which typically occurs at various times between the ages of six months and two-and-a-half years. During this stage, babies are learning their caregivers and others still exist, even when they can't see them. But since babies have no concept of time, they become anxious when their favorite people leave.[1]

---

1   Nemours Kids Health. (2023, March). *Separation anxiety.*
     https://kidshealth.org

Chapter Two: Separation Anxiety

1959 – 1964

My adoption at the age of two months reminds me of Moses when his mother placed him in a papyrus basket in the Nile. Pharaoh's daughter found him floating in the river unharmed and took him in. He was loved and nurtured until he became King of Egypt.

I was born November 9, 1959, at County Hospital in Tacoma, Washington on Pacific Avenue. My birth mother said they took me out of the room right away because her blood pressure was too high. The next day the nurse brought me into the room and told my birth mother to name me. She named me Candace. "You were the most beautiful baby I had ever seen," she said to me when we met years later.

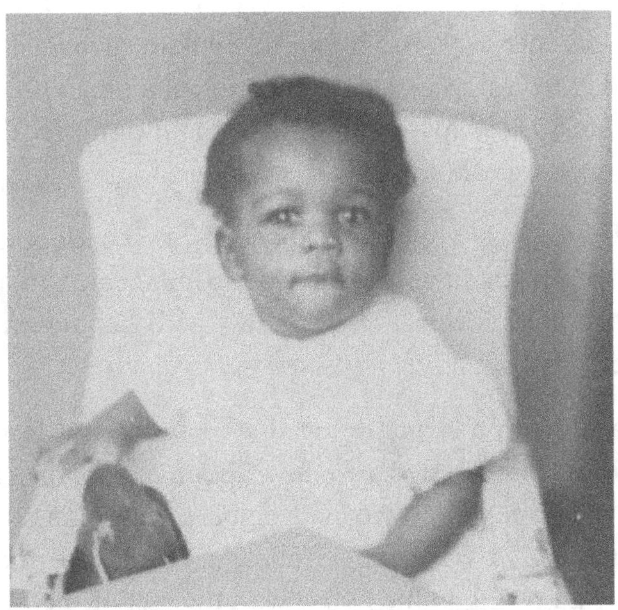

Photo of baby Sherri in 1960.

To the best of my knowledge, I was placed in foster care until my new parents picked me out of the bunch of crying babies. I can imagine the foster home getting me all freshened up with sweet-smelling soaps and lotions. I can see myself dressed in white lace with the pretty little white ruffled socks. They probably placed a ribbon around my small head of curly black hair. I lay in my little brown wooden crib waiting for someone to come and take me home, my eyes wide open looking around.

Back in the 60s foster parents weren't supposed to bond with the children, but when children are born they need to have touch from another human. Those touches are called stimuli. I can imagine how I was being fed, changed, and held by different people, just being passed around like a little rag doll waiting to be purchased by the next buyer. I never got the real affection I needed from my biological parents. Missing out on warmth, support, acceptance, and comfort was hard on me as it is for any child in that situation.

My new parents took me home to Spokane where I would be loved and cared for as God had planned all along. Of course, as a child I didn't know my adoption story and don't recall much of my life until I was about five years old.

One day, a young white lady knocked on our door carrying a dark brown bag like the doctors carried. She came in and sat on the brown couch. Mom said, "Would you like some tea?" but she declined.

I overheard the thin brunette social worker asking Mom all kinds of questions. She wanted to know about my brother and sister and a teenage nephew who had come from Mississippi to live with us because he was having trouble at home. She asked, "How is Gregory adjusting in the house with the rest of the family?"

I didn't hear all the questions because we had to stay in our rooms. We weren't allowed in grown people's conversations. That day always lingered in my head until some months later when my mom told me I was adopted.

School photo of Sherri around the time she said her first curse word, circa 1965.

When I was still five, I said my first curse word: "Shit."

Mom was nearby. "What did you say?"

"Shit," I repeated. I just thought it was a regular word I heard one of the neighbor boys say.

"Do you want me to wash your mouth out with soap?"

"No," I said with a quickness.

"That is a curse word and I dare you to say it again." Mom's word was final. My parents never cussed, drank, or smoked, and from that moment on I never said those words in their home again.

I'm sure there were increasing crimes in the Spokane neighborhood where we lived on the east side of town. Mom always wanted the best for us all so we ended up moving to the southeast side of town which is the Perry district. I started kindergarten at Grant School the year after we moved.

Photo of kindergarteners attending the Spokane Public Schools, circa 1965. Sherri is at the far right.

Did you know?

Even after the normal developmental stage of separation anxiety, adopted babies, preschoolers, school-age children, and even teenagers may have separation difficulties and other emotional problems related to being separated from their birth parents.[1] The Child Welfare Information Gateway offers a variety of publications to help adoptive parents learn how to ease their adopted child's anxieties and when to seek professional help.

---

1   Child Welfare Information Gateway. (n.d.). *Adoption and the stages of development.* Children's Bureau: Administration for Children and Families: U.S. Department of Health and Human Services. https://www.childwelfare.gov

Chapter Three: Home Alone

May 11, 1974

My dad was one of the kindest men anyone would ever meet. A tall man dressed in his sharp suit with Stacy Adams hat and shoes, he would be approached outside as we left the church service. People who smelled like alcohol would ask, "Can you spare some change?"

Dad would dig in his pocket, pull out some coins, and speak with the person about God. When I asked why he did that he said, "My dad told me to give when I could so I would be blessed." He taught me to live by that rule as well and I have seen many blessings from following it.

With Mom on her way to her meeting, Dad and I were left to hold down the fort, which we did quite well. When Mom was out of town, Dad always made breakfast for dinner on the weekends and it was the bomb.

Dad was a deacon in the church, so he was there every Saturday. This particular Saturday he had plans to go to the church we attended to do minor repairs to the men's bathroom and clean. Before leaving, he said, "While I'm gone you must not open the door for anyone."

What about relatives? Church members? Neighbors I know? I didn't think to ask him. At about 11:00 a.m., Dad made sure both the doors were locked. I could hear him open and close the front door, a solid one he installed when we moved in to keep us safe. Then he packed up his many tools, loaded them on his yellow-green pickup truck, and off he went.

I wasn't entirely alone because I had my mom's white poodle named Pepper as a companion. We often kept each other company when my parents weren't home. Pepper barked when someone would walk in front of our house to alert us someone was there, so I felt safe with him being in the house, especially when I was in my bedroom at the back of the house.

When I decided it was time to start sewing my Barbie dolls some new clothes, I got my shoe box out with different odds and ends in it like a needle, thread, and old material. During the week I had designed the clothes with models on paper, based on clothes my mother wore. Mom always matched up her outfits perfectly, with her hat, shoes, stockings in the right color, and a brooch. She often wore Liz Claiborne outfits for church on Sundays, and I would add to the design of her outfit when I made the Barbie dolls' clothes.

I didn't have a sewing machine, so I hand sewed everything. I had often watched Mom hem our clothes and sew buttons on when they fell off. Although I'm not sure where my material came from, my hand-sewn clothes were always nice. I even designed hats and purses to match for my Barbies. I had an eye for detail early on.

While I worked on my Barbie fashion project, I played my 1970s white Panasonic ball and chain AM radio. As I sewed, I could hear Michael Jackson and his brothers singing "ABC," "I Want You Back," "I'll Be There," and other great hits of the 70s.

I was having a good time home alone, when all of a sudden, I heard the doorbell ring. *Who's this? No one should be coming to the house. Otherwise, Dad would have told me. He warned me, "While I'm gone you must not open the door for anyone."*

Pepper was barking up a storm to alert me someone was at the door. Whoever was on the other side of the door must have heard Pepper barking. I stopped sewing and tip-toed down the hallway to see who was at the door. I snuck to the door and stood on my tiptoes to look through the rather high peephole. My dad was six feet tall, so I guess he didn't think of the short people in the family when he installed the peephole.

I was able to get a glance of who it was, my cousin Stan who was 28 years old and married with children. He was always coming over with my cousins to visit my mom, and my parents thought of him as a good family man. There he stood in his khaki pants, black shirt, and camel-colored jacket. I just knew he had my Lifesavers Storybook candy box he promised me for Christmas last year.

I immediately unlocked all the locks, forgetting about the conversation I had with my dad about not opening the door. I opened the big, deep-brown sturdy door and we spoke through the screen door which was locked. Then I unlocked the screen door to let Stan in.

Did you know?

While early elementary school boys are more likely to be sexually abused than older boys, girls become more vulnerable to sexual abuse as they reach adolescence.[1] Children and adolescents are vulnerable to sexual abuse because most perpetrators are known to the victim,[2] and most perpetrators are men,[1] who tend to be larger and can overpower a child. Although the data varies, studies find around half of the perpetrators are family members who are trusted by the child. These perpetrators take advantage of the family's trust by exploiting opportunities such as when children are unsupervised or their parents are busy.[1]

---

1   Hassan, M.A., Gary, F., Killion, C., Lewin, L., & Totten, V. (2015). Patterns of sexual abuse among children: Victims' and perpetrators' characteristics. *Journal of Aggression, Maltreatment & Trauma, 24,* 400 – 418. https://doi.10.1080/10926771.2015.1022289

2   National Children's Advocacy Center. (2018). *Child sexual abuse: Perpetrators, manipulation, disclosure, prevention.* https://www.nationalcac.org

Chapter Four: Lifesavers and Lunch

May 11, 1974

Stan came in and gave me the long-awaited Lifesavers Storybook candy box that was supposed to be for Christmas. "Thank you! Thank you!" I said. I jumped up and down with a big grin, so excited to finally get my candy box. My favorite was butterscotch. I would often take a roll of Lifesavers to church with me and secretly eat a piece when I thought no one was watching.

"Where are Uncle Everett and Auntie Vi?" Stan asked. His breath smelled like alcohol, but this was nothing unusual for him. He often came by like that.

"Mom is at a meeting and Dad went to the church to do some work," I said.

"Do you want to go to Dick's Hamburgers with me and your cousins for lunch?"

Who would turn down the best hamburgers and fries in town? And don't forget about the yummy tartar sauce. I said, "Yes," and walked down the hallway to put my shoes on and grab my house key. I was already dressed in a two-piece blue top and skirt with small flowers printed on it, just right for the spring weather.

I finished getting ready, grabbed my blue sweater, and stopped at the bathroom to look at my two ponytails. Next, I headed down the hallway and into the living room where I left Stan. We began to talk and out the door we went. I locked the house and walked down the long sidewalk to get in his car.

School photo of Sherri circa 1974.

As I approached the car, I saw my six-and-seven-year-old cousins sitting in the backseat. Happy as I could be, I walked in the street to get on the right side where my female cousin was sitting. As I opened the back passenger door, Stan said, "Get in the front seat." We were told to obey our elders so this naive girl did what I was told without hesitation.

Once in the front seat, I looked at Stan and he had an unusual smirk on his face. I turned to look back over the rather large seat and said to my cousins, "Hi."

They responded but not in a happy tone. That was the last conversation I had with them on the whole trip there and back.

Stan started the car and off we went to get burgers. *Why does he keep looking at me with his devilish smirk? Every time he comes to visit, he usually says hi and carries on with the conversation with my parents.*

We were four houses away from my house. *That's strange. Why is he touching my leg?* I kept looking at the houses as we went by. I sure wasn't trying to look at him.

Stan reached over and put his hand on my leg again. *What is going on? My dad never put his hand on my leg and neither did anyone else, for that matter.* I immediately thrust his hand away. It seemed like it became a game to him. The whole time he was talking up a storm, just making small talk about the weather, how fast I was growing up, and any other nonsense he could think of.

"Stop," I said over and over, but he wouldn't. By the time we had reached the end of my street, he had his hand under my skirt and his fingers in my panties. I kept thrusting his right hand away and saying, "Stop," but he continued. *I'm scared. This is making me feel sick.*

I felt overwhelmed, and my thoughts took me back to the last time I was afraid. *I haven't felt like this since I jumped off the back of my brother's bike a few years ago. I sprained my right arm in the process and had to go in the house and tell my mom the news, but I was not supposed to be on the back of my brother's bike. I had broken a rule and just knew I was going to get it. When I told Mom what happened she said, "I guess you got your punishment."*

Stan kept putting his fingers in my panties until he succeeded in moving them inside of my vagina, all the time with that wicked sneer on his face. I tried hard to push his hand away, but he pushed his fingers more forcefully into my vagina. I squirmed around so he would stop, but he continued assaulting me.

I want my mom and wish I would have listened to my dad. "Don't open the door," he said. Why did I open the door? Why?

As we were getting closer to Dick's Hamburgers, I was hoping to see someone I knew so I could get in the car with them and tell them what was going on. There was always a familiar face there; it was one of the most popular places in town, but this day I saw no one I knew.

"Stay in the car while I order lunch," Stan said. When he got out of the car, I looked in the backseat at my cousins. They just looked straight ahead and didn't say a word.

This is confusing. He keeps talking, so why aren't they saying anything? We always play together. I'm angry—not at them but at myself because I should not have opened the door. Why didn't I listen to my dad? Why?

Dad is literally two blocks from Dick's on the right side of the street at the church on East Third Avenue. Maybe he was outside putting the sprinklers on the grass when we drove by … I hope he saw me and will do something so I can get away from this monster. I'm so scared that I don't think I'll be able to eat.

Stan came back to the car with the food that usually smelled so good, but today it smelled like death. My body was just numb to what was going on. We pulled out of the parking lot of Dick's. *There's that evil smirk again.*

Once we got close to the church he sped up. My hand was on the door handle. *I can escape if I open the door and jump. No, I don't have the nerve.*

My dad was nowhere in sight. He must have been inside the church because all I saw was his yellow-green truck sitting there on the side of the church.

Ooooo, my stomach is knotted, feels like I want to throw up. The food in the car doesn't smell appetizing. What is Stan talking about? My mind is shut down where I can't concentrate. I just want to go home.

I imagine the little bird I found lying on the ground just wished he would have stayed low in his nest. I'm sure when the bird fell, he was looking over the edge of his nest, and being too young to fly, he fell to the ground. I'm sure he just wanted to see his mother. All I want is my mother.

Did you know?

The child advocacy organization Darkness to Light explains perpetrators of child sexual abuse use a technique called *grooming* to gain the child's trust.[1] While giving presents can be a harmless and loving gesture, grooming often includes special treatment like giving gifts, taking the child on outings, or offering the child's favorite foods. The perpetrator may test the child's boundaries by touching them in inappropriate ways, so they can determine whether the child will resist before escalating their behavior. Or they may try to get the child alone so no one can intervene in the abuse. For a thorough explanation of grooming and red-flag behaviors, check out the resource referenced below.

---

1   Darkness to Light. (n.d.). *Grooming and red flag behaviors.*
    https://www.d2l.org

Chapter Five: Don't Tell Anyone

May 11, 1974

We were getting closer to my house, and I just wanted to get out of his car and get inside where I should have been in the first place. As we were heading down my street, which is quite curvy on East Fifth Avenue, I started to get a glimpse of my house.

We are finally here at my house. I can get out of Stan's car, say goodbye, get into my house and lock my door, never to open any door again.

I hurriedly got out of the car, said goodbye to my cousins, and closed the door. *There is no way I'm saying bye to him, he is just up to no good.* I walked up the first set of stairs leading from the sidewalk up to our front yard, only to see Stan getting out of his car. I sped up my pace but got a glimpse of Stan right behind me. I thought maybe the kids had gotten out of the car to eat lunch but they were nowhere in sight.

Where is he going? I don't need him to open the door for me. I just want him to go get back in his car.

My house key was in hand. At this point standing at the top of the steps to the house, I thought to myself, *Dad you have too many locks on the door.* I fumbled with the locks, first on the storm door and then the main door. *Stan is talking to me, Lord knows about what. Just let me get these locks open faster and get in the house, so he can go away.*

I finally got the last lock unlocked and myself into the house. *Why is he still trying to come in? Things are getting ready to be ugly, all over a one-dollar Lifesavers Storybook candy box.*

Stan closed the front door and pushed me up against the wall. He began to kiss me and his hands were all over the place. I steadily said, "No," and I tried to push him away but he was probably 5'9" to my little frame of only 80 pounds. His kisses became harder as he began to rub his hard penis on me through my clothes. I tried with all my might to push him away but nothing worked. A tear rolled down my face as if that was going to help. *I'm scared but I don't know what to do.*

Stan picked me up and placed me on the floor right at the front door. He began grinding on me along with the unwanted kisses that smelled like stale beer. He raised me up enough to pull my panties off, he was so heavy I couldn't really move. He began to unzip his pants and I could feel he had pulled his penis out.

The next thing I knew he was pushing it into my virgin vagina. As I lay there looking at the front door with tears rolling down my cheek, he did his nasty deed. *What the hell just happened with my cousin on me like this?*

After he finished his dirt, he got off me and pulled his pants up. I stood up shaking and pulled my skirt down in shame. My panties lay on our green carpet. Pepper was yapping. *Even the dog can sense something is wrong.* I didn't try to stop him from barking.

Stan grabbed me by my little frail arm and pushed me up against the wall by the door. "Don't tell anyone." His voice told me he meant business, so I was scared to move or say anything.

Stan smoothed his short afro, found his way out, and I locked the doors up. I was shaking, scared half to death. *What to do? I don't know.*

I walked down the semi-dark hallway and into my once-cheerful bedroom. I was detached from all my surroundings, nothing made sense to me. I didn't hear the birds chirping, just silence. It seemed as though everything had come to a wrenching halt, all in a matter of seconds.

I took off all my clothes in my room and headed into the bathroom to take a shower. I turned the water on as hot as I could and got inside. The water sprinkled on me, getting hotter, rushing down my little naked body. *I just want all that wet stuff inside of me to be gone.*

The water got hotter and hotter but I didn't care, I was just numb. There was so much steam in the bathroom. My mind played over and over what had happened to me. I didn't know if I wanted to laugh or cry. I didn't have a name for the emotions I was dealing with at the time. I got out of the shower dripping wet, put my clothes back on, and hoped my dad would notice something was different about me.

Nowadays we know we need DNA to charge anyone. I wanted it erased completely but that's not how life works. You can't erase, scrub, or disinfect when you are violated like that. It's like a scar you get; sometimes it will go away depending on how deep the scar is. Other times the scar is with you for life.

Dad got home an hour later, came in, and didn't notice I wasn't the same little girl. I didn't realize I had lost my virginity to rape that day because Mom never talked to me about the birds and the bees. Dad and I ate dinner, watched TV, and prepared to go to bed after talking with Mom. *She'll be home from her trip tomorrow, which is Sunday. I know she will see something is not right with me.*

Did you know?

Child sexual assaults are extremely under-reported, and this is so for many reasons. Estimates of disclosure range from 16%[1] to 26%[2] of child sexual abuse victims who reported their assaults to a caregiver or other trusted adult. Children may not understand what has happened or they may not have the vocabulary to explain it. Child victims tend to be frightened of telling about the experience because perpetrators usually warn them to keep the sexual abuse a secret and often threaten the child, their family, or their pets. The child may be embarrassed, afraid they won't be believed, think it's their fault, or fear they will get in trouble for what happened.[1]

Once an adult has been informed of the abuse, only about half of the caregivers notify the authorities. When police become involved, just one in five cases is ever prosecuted, and only about half of those cases result in convictions.[2]

---

1   National Children's Advocacy Center. (2018). *Child sexual abuse: Perpetrators, manipulation, disclosure, prevention.*
    https://www.nationalcac.org

2   Darkness to Light. (n.d.). *Reporting child sexual abuse.*
    https://www.d2l.org

Chapter Six: What is Going on with My Body?

May 12, 1974

Morning came and what used to be exciting for me to hear in the morning wasn't. *The birds are chirping but I just want my mom to fix what Stan has done to me. I want my nerves and this frightful feeling to go away. Can someone please explain to me what is going on in my body? My mind won't let me move on from yesterday.*

Sunday seemed like just a regular day, but it was different because I didn't have any interest in playing with my dolls. I just sat on the back porch wanting my sister who had left home years earlier.

Mom came home Sunday evening, and I was so excited to see her. We helped her unload the car and Dad asked her questions about the women's meeting. Mom had a good time as usual but she didn't notice something had happened to me.

All that evening I tried to make Mom notice I needed her but she was probably too tired. I stood in front of her and followed her around to no avail. All kinds of things were going on in my head for the first time in my life. I hated Stan for what he had done, which I was still trying to figure out. I didn't know what hate felt like until that tragic day.

This was also the first time I kept a secret from my parents, thanks to Stan. *I really want to tell them, but will they believe me over their nephew, or better yet an adult?*

Nighttime was fast approaching and I had to prepare to go to school. My anxiety was kicking in, so I felt nervous and my thoughts would race. *I don't really want to go to school because*

I'll have to walk. Stan drives the route I walk and I'm afraid I may run into him again.

I climbed into my warm bed and immediately pulled the covers over my head, not sure what that was going to do. I was trying to turn my brain off but it just played what had happened over and over. I eventually went to sleep.

Monday morning arrived and it was time to get up for school. The sounds of birds used to be fun to listen to, but they were just noise in the wind now. I climbed out of bed and looked back at my sheets because I felt something cold and wet. To my surprise, I saw a bunch of blood on my once-white sheets. I looked at my pajamas and they were bloody, too. *Oh my gosh, what did Stan do? How am I going to explain to my mom that Stan did this? I am afraid to even say anything to her. This is my fault. What will be the consequences?*

I went into the bathroom to get a wet rag with the hope that I could clean up the blood. I only made matters worse, smearing it and making a bigger mess out of the situation. I finally got the courage to go out and tell my mom I was bleeding.

I walked down the hall and into the kitchen where Mom was making her favorite cup of Folgers coffee. "Mom," I said, "I'm bleeding." I was shaking.

Mom looked at me. "You started your period."

"Period? What is that?" No one had explained anything to me about menstruation, but at least her answer told me I wasn't going to be in trouble.

Mom said, "Get cleaned up so we can go to the store and get your sanitary products." I still had no clue because that's all she said, but it sounded OK to me. *It must be something Stan did. Now what do I do? This is one more thing on my plate.*

We went to the store around 7:00 a.m. and then came home so I could finish getting ready for school. Once ready for school, I had to walk in all four seasons, no matter what the weather was like. I hated this part of spring when the gnats came out because they would fly up my nose, so I remember walking fast just to avoid them. *I definitely don't want to see Stan in the mess I'm in. I am not going to get in the car with him.*

Day after day, I trudged to school through the month of May. The pain and trauma I endured on that horrific Saturday afternoon were still fresh, and I was having a hard time focusing on my schoolwork. I used to answer questions in class, but now I became mute. I stared into space quite often, just wanting to get back home where I felt safe. My grades, which were *A*s and *B*s, began to drop because I couldn't concentrate.

Did you know?

Children think their parents are all-knowing and all-powerful. Even adolescents can hang onto the myth of "mothers know everything." Child victims may believe their mother knows about the sexual abuse or that she can notice something is different. When the mother fails to recognize what has happened, the child may assume she does know but doesn't care.[1]

In households where the parents don't educate children about their bodies, children can be especially vulnerable. The National Children's Advocacy Center recommends for parents to be proactive in teaching children the proper names for body parts (including genitals) and if someone touches them in a sexual way it is not the child's fault.[2] In addition, children should be taught about healthy versus unhealthy touch, that no one should touch their private parts, and that they have the right to refuse a hug or other contact, no matter who the person is. Parents should frequently reinforce to their children that it is safe to discuss sex and sexual abuse.[3]

---

1   Mothers of Sexually Abused Children (MOSAC). (n.d.). *Child risk factors*. https://www.mosac.net

2   National Children's Advocacy Center. (2018). *Child sexual abuse: Perpetrators, manipulation, disclosure, prevention.* https://www.nationalcac.org

3   Mothers of Sexually Abused Children (MOSAC). (n.d.). *25 things parents should know about sexual abuse.* https://www.mosac.net

Chapter Seven: The Minister

June 5, 1974

One morning near the end of the school year, as I was walking to school about one block from our house, I noticed a car pulling up on the other side of the street. *I hope it's not Stan. Oh, it's one of the ministers in our church. That's a relief!* This was someone my parents invited over to our house for Sunday dinner and weekly visits.

Clinton, the minister, was probably in his late 30s. After he stopped the car he asked, "Do you want a ride?"

"Sure," I said. I walked across the street to get in the car with the golden-skinned young man. I assumed since he and his wife were good friends of my parents, he was going to take me right to school. *I just want to get off the streets, away from Stan, and get to school where I feel safe.*

"Good morning," I said.

We were supposed to go straight down Fifth Avenue to get to my school. As we approached Sherman Street we stopped at the stop sign, and I heard his signal come on. *Now why would he turn his signal on when the school is straight ahead?* When Clinton turned right, I knew something was wrong. *Why is this happening again? Can I get out of this car?*

Clinton took me to his apartment somewhere on the north side of town where he and his wife lived. When we arrived, I felt frozen, numb; I followed him without speaking. He took me inside the house to a room that was well-lit by the sun coming through one window. The curtains were green with yellow sheers and there were lots of unpacked boxes everywhere.

I was leaning next to a box when Clinton began to fondle my genitals. He had the same smirk on his face as Stan did, so I knew he was up to no good.

Clinton took his penis out and got closer to me as he was moving his hand up and down. He tried to put it inside my vagina but I was determined that was not going to happen to me again. I clamped down as hard as I could, which I guess was a turn-off for him. He made me rub his hard penis while he looked in this magazine with naked women and men.

This was my first exposure to porn; he had a box full.

Clinton pulled my head towards him and down to his penis, which he pushed past my lips just before he spilled his semen into my mouth. *What is this warm liquid in my mouth? I just want to spit it out. When will this all be over?*

Clinton left and went into the bathroom across the hall, brought me a wet towel, and then went back into the bathroom. I wiped the side of my mouth off and laid the rag down on a box.

Clinton came back in the room and it was time to go. We got in the car. What we spoke about, I don't recall as I must have been in shock.

I just want to get to school and away from this awful man. This is so confusing. Why is this happening again? What did I do to bring this on myself?

We pulled up at school where I got out of his car and went inside. At this point I was late for school and had to get a late pass. After Stan raped me, I became skilled at making up lies about why I was late for school or why I needed to leave early. No one ever questioned me because I was always in school.

I went into my second-period classroom and just sat there, inattentive as to what was going on. *No one notices I have been sexually abused, and I'm afraid of what will happen if I tell on these men. I just want my life to be over.*

Later, I remember going to church and having to see Clinton in the pulpit preaching God's word. *His behavior is not what I was taught in Sunday school and church,* I would think. Clinton would try to approach me after church, but I would immediately turn and go in the opposite direction to avoid him. *He always has that smirk on his face when I look at him.* Sunday dinners never included him or his wife again—they always said they had something to do, and as far as I knew, Mom never questioned it.

I started making up excuses not to go to church so I wouldn't have to look at Clinton sitting in the pulpit with a smirk on his face. Sometimes I would say, "Sorry, Mom, I have to study for a test." Other times my excuse would be, "I have a lot of homework to do."

"Why didn't you finish it at school?" Mom would ask.

I hate lying to Mom, but what am I supposed to do? I sure don't want to look at him. "I don't know, I just didn't finish it."

Did you know?

The Centers for Disease Control reports children who are sexually abused are at risk for further victimization. In fact, girls who have been sexually abused have a 2-13 times greater risk of being sexually abused again in the future. Not only that but also the risk of future intimate partner violence (non-sexual) is doubled.[1]

---

1   Centers for Disease Control and Prevention (CDC). (2022, April 6). *Fast facts: Preventing child sexual abuse.* https://www.cdc.gov

Chapter Eight: Too Old for Dolls and Too Young to Date

1974

My progress in school began to suffer because my mind was all over the place. By the time I started my freshman year in high school, I didn't comprehend a thing, and I would rather stay home and be by myself. I began smoking with my friends Paulette, Francesca, and S.E., just to belong with the group. Every chance we got, we were outside at the back of the school.

Sherri's ninth grade school photo, circa 1975.

On a typical school day, we'd meet behind the school during our lunch break. Francesca, S.E., and I would smoke our Kools, while my best friend Paulette would start dishing her gossip. "You won't believe who I was with last night," she said as she took a sip of the beer she'd snuck in her purse.

S.E. knelt to tie the laces of her Converses. "Pass that beer and then tell us." She reached for it with one hand.

Francesca's eyes twinkled. "It better not be that reject from fifth period," she said. I burst out laughing. Francesca always made me forget my problems with a joke about someone we didn't like.

Everyone in our little group had a story to tell about the night before, but I didn't share much of anything. *What am I going to say? They're allowed to date, have boyfriends, and wear make-up, stockings, and high heels, while my parents are still treating me like a child. Besides, the ones I trusted betrayed me. I'm sure if I tell them what happened to me it will be all over the school and my church.*

One night during my sophomore year, I snuck out to a friend's house where her dad was having a card party. I wore the tight jeans, bandana, and high heels Paulette brought to school for me so I would have a cool outfit to wear. S.E., Francesca, and Paulette were there, too, already drinking and flirting with older men even though we were only 16.

"Hey, foxy lady." A clean-shaven, tall, handsome brown-skinned man a few years my senior was talking to me. "I'm Lew. I don't think we've met before."

"I'm Sherri. Nice to meet you."

We connected and started hanging out, although I could only see him while I was supposed to be at school. Lew would pick me up

Photo of Sherri Jones as a teen, circa 1977.

from high school when he was off work from his post in the military, and we would go over to his friend's house to have sex and a little bit of T.J. Swann.

When I started drinking more alcohol, my mom never noticed. I climbed out of my bedroom window to go hang out with my friends at house parties, got wasted, and allowed strange men to kiss and touch me. Back in the day, slow dancing was the thing, so I experienced all types of different men bumping and grinding on me.

By the time I was a junior, after a few slow dances with some men who were rather aggressive, I always had an intuition about the men who were safe to slow dance with. I would say no to the ones who gave me a bad feeling. I learned how to push them away, say "no," and mean it.

Mom never noticed I was changing right in front of her, sometimes I was angry because she didn't. I just wanted somebody—anybody—to help me make the pain go away.

Did you know?

Children and adolescents who have been sexually abused almost always experience mental health consequences and behavior changes. Victims may feel as if the assault was somehow their fault, and/or they may experience anxiety, self-blame, and trust issues.[1] In addition, they can develop post-traumatic stress disorder, anxiety disorders, depression, and eating disorders.[2] Behavior changes may include sleep problems, irritability, anger outbursts, neglecting personal hygiene, withdrawal from friends and family, smoking, alcohol and substance abuse, self-harm, risky sexual activity, running away, and unusual weight gain/loss or other unhealthy eating patterns.[3] Young victims not only experience these mental health and behavioral issues but also they may have difficulty concentrating or lose motivation, causing their academic performance to suffer.[4]

---

1   Crawford-Jakubiak, J. E., et al. (2017). Care of the adolescent after an acute sexual assault. *Pediatrics, 139*(3), e20164243.
    https://doi.org/10.1542/peds.2016-4243

2   Banvard-Fox, C. (2020). Sexual assault in adolescents. *Primary Care, 47*(2), 331-349. https://doi.org/10.1016/j.pop.2020.02.010

3   Child Welfare Information Gateway. (n.d.). *Parenting a child or youth who has been sexually abused: A guide for foster and adoptive parents.* Children's Bureau: Administration for Children and Families: U.S. Department of Health and Human Services.
    https://www.childwelfare.gov

4   Emerson Hospital 2018 Youth Risk Behavior Survey, cited in Banvard-Fox, C., et al. (2020). Sexual assault in adolescents. *Primary Care, 47*(2), 331-349. https://doi.org/10.1016/j.pop.2020.02.010

Chapter Nine: On My Own Too Soon

1977

My relationship with Lew lasted until I was in my senior year of high school when the military transferred him. Once he left, I felt lonely and was looking for anyone to fill the void.

Before I finished my senior year, I moved away from home and ended up staying with three sisters who had just lost their mother some months prior. We all got along and we helped one another finish school. Until I moved in with my friends, I never knew what freedom was. There was no curfew or anyone telling us what to do. We rented a one-bedroom apartment but all managed to stay in our lanes.

On my first Thanksgiving there with them, we had a good day. I prepared the turkey for the occasion. My dad often showed up with leftovers for us to eat, and we were always grateful.

It was in my soul to dance, so I started hanging out at the Sheraton Hotel. Although I was only 18, I was able to get in because I used a driver's license belonging to a friend who was 21. I may have looked like her, but my maturity was definitely not there. Looking back, it seems like I was always placed in the crowd with older people. My feet were always dancing around, and I was having a ball being in the atmosphere of older men. I pretended to be mature, so I acted like being in a club with older guys was nothing.

One night when I went out to the Sheraton, they were playing old-school music. I met a well-spoken, handsome guy named Pete who bought me a couple of drinks. I didn't realize it at the time but he was 25 and I was 19 years old, like the song "Age Ain't Nothing but a Number" by Aaliyah. We danced the night away, and after the club, we went to Denny's. Like my previous boyfriend, he was also in the military; within two weeks we were dating. He would come downtown after he finished work and we would hang out. I thought I was falling in love with someone who loved me, too.

Pete and I did everything together. Sometimes while he was at work, I would go with him to sit in the lobby and watch him work. He worked for the billeting office, which is where all the military came for a place to stay once they got to the base. It was like a hotel but strictly for the military and their spouses. We also went to the movies quite a bit and enjoyed driving the streets to sightsee and be with each other.

After dating for about a year, one day when we were making love, I felt something had happened within my body because it felt different than any other time we had sex. He left, but in my spirit, I knew something was not right.

I called my mom. "Guess what? I had a dream about a ghost."

"A ghost?" Mom said. "Are you pregnant?"

"No, I don't think so …"

But Mom knew I had the dream because something felt strange. In her wisdom, she said, "You may want to go to the doctor."

She was right. I finally went to get checked, and the doctor said, "You are pregnant and your baby is due in October."

Wow, a baby. What am I going to do with a baby at 19 years old? My whole world is going to change. How am I supposed to tell Pete I'm having his baby?

When Pete came over that evening I gave him the news. To my surprise, he was excited about it. He called his mom on the phone and told her about the baby, and then passed me the phone. After the phone call to his mother, he said he wanted to marry me. I was overjoyed with the news because I had no clue how to care for a baby, let alone myself at times.

As the weeks went on, Pete received orders to go to the Philippines. I thought I was going, but he never mentioned marriage again, much less bringing me along. He provided me with money and his car, but I was left all alone to figure out this thing called motherhood. He came back years later, but by that time distance had separated us. I was so hurt and my trust issues with people were just getting deeper.

Did you know?

A potential consequence of sexual abuse is that the adolescent victim will develop pseudomature behaviors, engaging in activities they believe make them mature when in fact they are not developmentally ready.[1] Some examples of pseudomature behaviors include precocious sexual activity or romantic involvements, and minor delinquency, such as skipping school, shoplifting, smoking, drinking, and substance abuse.[2] These pseudomature adolescents are more likely to engage in risky sexual behavior and have unintended pregnancies. In addition, victims of sexual abuse have more than double the risk of becoming teen mothers when compared with other adolescents.[3]

---

1   Crosson-Tower, C. (2010). Cited in Safe Kids Thrive. (2017). *Recognizing abuse and its effects.* https://safekidsthrive.org

2   Allen, J. P., et al. (2014 Sept). What ever happened to the 'cool' kids? Long-term sequelae of early adolescent pseudomature behavior. *Child Development, 85*(5), 1866–1880. https://doi.org.10.1111/cdev.12250

3   Auman-Bauer, K. (2018 Sept. 11). *New research shows sexual abuse unique risk factor for teenage pregnancy.* Penn State. https://www.psu.edu

Chapter Ten: Post-partum Depression
1979

After I got pregnant, I moved to another apartment by myself. I had my son Shawn in October and had to figure out how to be a mother without Pete or my friends there to support me. When I got out of the hospital I stayed at my parents' house so my mom could help me. I was able to get some sleep for about a week while I rested there.

This lasted until my breast milk came in and shot across the breakfast table. My shirt was soaking wet from breast milk, and Mom had to give me towels to put in my bra. I was so embarrassed to be around Dad that I decided to go back to my apartment.

My body was going through another change and I wasn't sure what was going on. Even though I had done everything I was told to help with nursing, nothing worked. I was struggling to nurse my son and was so frustrated I was ready to throw in the towel. Shawn did not want to latch on to my breast and I had no clue how to nurse. I became very depressed during this time but I knew I had to take care of my son.

Shawn was vomiting up his formula milk, so we went back and forth to the doctor's office. He became so sick with colic the doctor prescribed special sleeping arrangements to prevent the reflux that was making him so miserable. Each night, I had to place him on a board at a 45-degree angle with his legs spraddled around a pole in the middle to keep him from sliding down.

These days, devices similar to this are well-padded with thick, soft straps, but Shawn's board looked so uncomfortable. Seeing him like that was awful, especially at night when he should have been in his nice warm bed. I had him sleep right next to my bed just to make sure he wasn't choking on his milk. At times I would put the board with Shawn on it in my bed just to be close to him, but I realized I might accidentally knock him off the bed and have a bigger problem. I don't think I got much sleep for the two months Shawn had to sleep on this board.

Then God sent me an angel. I met Mercedes and became friends with her in the hospital when our sons were born around the same time. I told her my story about my son being unable to keep his milk down, and she offered to nurse him for me. Ten years my senior, Mercedes was an inspiration to me on things I needed help with, like recuperating after having my child. She moved in with me in November, helped me pay rent and buy groceries, and showed me how to do things like perm my hair. My son was able to tolerate her breast milk and began to gain weight every month. I was very thankful and I'm sure my son was, too.

After a few months, Mercedes had to go to Germany to be with her husband who was stationed there for military duty. She started packing little by little and in April of 1980, I was once again going to be without a good friend. I never realized how mothers can be a blessing to other mothers who are unable to nurse their children when there is a need like that. I am forever grateful my friend Mercedes was in my life at that time. Forty-three years later she is still considered my big sister from another mother.

When Mercedes left I had another void in my life that brought on separation anxiety. Now my almost-one-year-old son was the only person living with me in my apartment. Since my son didn't cry a lot, my apartment was especially silent. We made it through by watching TV, and I read books to Shawn quite a bit.

I gained a new friend when my neighbor LuAnn, who lived downstairs from me, started to communicate with me more. LuAnn was six years older than me, sported dishwater blonde hair, and she had four beautiful children. Her oldest daughter Cindy took a liking to me, so she was always nearby when I would go downstairs.

LuAnn took me in and continued to nourish me where Mercedes left off with my son, especially helping with his reflux problem. She would cook some delicious meals such as mac and cheese, fried chicken, and other dishes. When she cooked, I would be right in the kitchen with her to see how she prepared food because I wasn't the best cook. Back when I was living at home, Mom didn't want anybody in the kitchen with her, so I always watched her work from a distance.

I didn't have a car at the time, so LuAnn would always ask me the night before if I wanted to go grocery shopping with her. Of course, I would say yes and we would have a good time shopping and laughing. Since she was the oldest of the girls and old enough to watch her siblings, Cindy would watch Shawn, too.

My apartment in Spokane on East Second Street was on a little dirt road, and it was fine for a while, but then one night a peeping Tom climbed onto my balcony on the second floor. All I could see through the kitchen window was his shadowy figure wearing dark clothes. I was scared to pieces, but somehow he fell and hit the ground with a loud thud.

When I told Dad, he said, "You'll need to move to a better neighborhood." Just like when Mom moved our family to a safer neighborhood, I had to pack my bags and do the same for Shawn.

Did you know?

Studies consistently demonstrate that women who were sexually assaulted in childhood have higher rates and greater degrees of anxiety and depression during pregnancy.[1,2,3]Both established and newer research proves childhood sexual abuse correlates with postpartum depression as well.[1,3] When a new mother is depressed, she may be unable to bond properly with her child; furthermore, she may not be equipped to support her child's emotional development. As a result, healthcare providers need to actively screen for risk factors of depression such as childhood trauma to prevent long-term problems with maternal mental health, the mother's relationship with her child(ren), and her child(ren)'s emotional development.[1]

---

1   Buist, A., & Janson, H. (2001). Childhood sexual abuse, parenting, and postpartum depression - A 3-year follow-up study. *Child Abuse & Neglect*, *25*(7), 909-21. https://doi.org./10.1016/S0145-2134(01)00246-0

2   Wosu, A. C., Gelaye, B., & Williams, M. A. (2015). History of childhood sexual abuse and risk of prenatal and postpartum depression or depressive symptoms: An epidemiologic review. *Archive of Women's Mental Health*, *18*(5), 659-671. https://doi.org/10.1007/s00737-015-0533-0

3   Belete, H., Eyaya, M. & Mihret, M. S. (2020). The effect of early childhood sexual abuse on mental health among postpartum women visiting public health facilities in Bahir Dar City, Ethiopia: Multicenter study. *International Journal of Women's Health*, *12*, 1271-1281. https://doi.org./10.2147/IJWH.S283924

Chapter Eleven: Pregnant Again

1983

Shawn and I moved into our first newly built four-plex apartment on Thor. I was so happy to be living in a rather new apartment complex that was way better than my other places. I met a young lady named Catherine who, among other things we had in common, had a son the same age as Shawn, so we became good friends. She told me stories about her life with guys and how she overcame certain bad relationships.

Catherine taught me how to make Indian fry bread, a dish of the indigenous people, and other delicious native foods. She also took me to my very first Native American pow-wow, which was in Coeur d'Alene, Idaho. I was intrigued by the dancing, the beautiful headdresses, and the outfits. I had not experienced anything like it before.

One day Catherine asked, "Do you want to go to the NCO Club at the Air Base?" She had the most beautiful smile.

"Yes, of course," I said. We got dressed, left Shawn with some friends, and off we went to do a little dancing and have some cocktails.

Catherine didn't drink but she sure did have a good time. *I thought the only way to have fun was to drink and not think about the pain I experienced from being raped.*

"How do you not drink when you go out?" I remember asking her. She said she just didn't need to drink to be happy.

This particular night I met a handsome, 5'9", brown-skinned, well-groomed, and fresh-smelling young man named Terrance.

We started dating and my friends told me we were a good-looking couple. Terrance would catch the bus from the Air Force base to visit me and stay for the weekend to get a break from the barracks.

Terrance was a chef who loved to cook, and I was ready to eat what was prepared. I would invite my family over for card parties and they would all bring a dish to share. We would have a great time laughing, listening to music, and playing cards.

Gradually, I noticed Terrance was drinking more and more alcohol. He would be distant from my family and then once they left, he would flip the switch and say things that didn't make sense. One night after my cousins left, he got so upset, he threw an Old English 800 bottle down on the tile floor. I was barefoot and tried to get out of the way, but I stepped on the jagged glass and it lodged in the back of my ankle. The gash was so bad I had to get stitches. To this day I have a scar as a reminder of what happened that awful night.

One morning not long after this, I had some news for him. "Terrance, I'm pregnant," I said.

"That's fine," he said, "but I want to make sure you give the baby my last name."

I already decided if I have more children they will have the same last name as me, and he is showing signs of violence. "I think it's best for you to move on," I said.

Terrance had to be at work on Monday, so he left and did not come back. Baby Daddy Number Two was gone.

Friends who don't judge you and love you unconditionally are hard to come by, but things were changing. Catherine found a new place so she packed up and moved, leaving me alone with my separation anxiety once again.

I was working for the East Central Community Center information desk. My job was to help people find places that would pay their rent or food banks and other essential human services. I enjoyed my job because I liked helping people, but the Center eventually closed due to financial problems. I felt so isolated with no one to talk to about how I was feeling about Shawn, my pregnancy, and the now-absent Terrance. It was depressing, not only because I felt lonely but also because I wasn't sure how I would take care of my son and the baby I was expecting.

My name came up on the Spokane housing list, so I had an opportunity to find a better place to live. I searched for an apartment or a house relentlessly and finally met with an older gentleman who had a two-bedroom house on the east side of town. I told him my situation and why I needed to move, but the only problem was my voucher for housing didn't meet what he wanted for rent. God provided, and the man adjusted his rent price so I could meet the qualification for housing. The Housing Authority set up an appointment for inspection, the house passed, and I got the keys to my first home in 1983.

The house's exterior was mint green; the interior had two bedrooms and wood paneling on the walls which meant it would be somewhat warm in the winter and was just the right size for me and my son. The house also had a small yard for my son to play in and no noise from other tenants since it was a single-family home.

On moving day, Dad showed up with a surprise. "What's that in your truck?" I said.

It was Mom and Dad's old washer and dryer. "We got a new set, so you can have these," he said.

"Thanks, Dad," I said. "You always come through when I need you. I'm so thankful for no more laundry-mats." *I know he's getting tired of moving us.*

My dad unloaded his truck with our belongings, said his good-bye, and left. Shawn and I unpacked our things and made our house a home.

I was so thankful to be moving into my own house closer to family and friends who were in the area. My parents lived about 10 minutes from me so I was feeling somewhat safe again knowing they were close by. My brother lived two houses over from me so that was special, too. Robertus was a truck driver and would always stop by in his truck to check on me and grab something to eat.

Living close to family gave me a sense of connection I hadn't had in a while. I was starting to feel safe again in my own skin. I was able to relax just knowing my brother was close and all I had to do was make a call and he would be there.

Shawn was off to kindergarten and was doing extremely well in school. He even won a couple of contests they had at his school. He also met one of his best friends, Ricky.

Ricky's parents always took Shawn with them on their family camping trips. I mentioned a couple of times to his parents that I didn't have money for Shawn to go, but they always reassured me he would be taken care of and didn't need anything. It wasn't often that I let him go off with others for the weekend, but I felt very comfortable with them. These boys were inseparable and are still friends to date.

Shawn would come back home and tell me about his camping adventures and be ready to go again. I am forever grateful he was able to experience life outside of what I was able to provide for him.

Being on housing assistance meant my rent was paid but I still had a utility bill and had to buy necessities for the house and clothes for my son for school. I may have had $300 left over plus the $100 in food stamps which went quickly.

I had no child support for Shawn because I didn't know how and where to apply for it. Pete had gone overseas to the Philippines and I was clueless. Someone told me who to call but when I did, I had no information on him and they weren't trying to help. It was a dead end so I gave up searching. If it wasn't for my dad bringing leftover food, we would not have made it. There were times when I would go to bed without eating so my son could eat. After all, I had a growing boy in kindergarten to take care of.

The Green Shanty Shack where Sherri lived in 1983.

I went out to the NCO Club on the base and met lots of people I could relate to. Before long, my house became the party house on Madelia Street. We called it the Green Shanty Shack. I always had people knocking on my door to visit, especially the military guys.

I had tried weed early on after I was raped, but it didn't sit well with my inner spirit. Even though I wasn't a smoker of weed, the guys who partied at my house would ask me to hold on to it for them when they would return to base. I would keep it for them, and they would always return the favor by bringing me food for the kids or a bottle of alcohol from the base.

I never once thought I could have gone to jail for holding onto their weed, and I didn't even smoke. After a while I stopped holding on to their care packages because I didn't want anything to happen to my son.

Terrance still called to check on me, but I wanted no part of his unwelcome behavior even though I had his seed growing within me. I felt sick throughout my whole pregnancy, probably from my nerves. In 1984, I gave birth to a healthy baby boy I named Bradford.

Did you know?

Intimate partner violence (IPV), when a partner or spouse intentionally causes emotional, sexual, or physical harm, is a public health issue that affects 25% of women and 14% of men in relationships.[1] To combat the harms of IPV, researchers need to understand its origins, and research in the last 25 years has pointed to childhood maltreatment as a primary contributor to a person's victimization by or perpetration of IPV. A 2015 study examined how IPV in adults correlates with many types of childhood maltreatment, including neglect, physical abuse, and sexual abuse. The results indicated any form of childhood maltreatment increases the likelihood a person will experience being a perpetrator, victim, or reciprocal participant in IPV. In addition, an experience of childhood sexual abuse significantly increases the risk the adult survivor will be a victim of IPV.[2]

---

1   Breiding, M. J., Black, M. C., & Ryan, G. W. (2008). Prevalence and risk factors of intimate partner violence in eighteen US states/territories, 2005. *American Journal of Preventive Medicine, 34*(2), 112-118. https://doi.org/10.1016/j.amepre.2007.10.001

2   McMahon, K., Hoertel, N., Wall, M. M., Okuda, M., Limosin, F., & Blanco, C. (2015). Childhood maltreatment and risk of intimate partner violence: A national study. *Journal of Psychiatric Research, 69*, 42-49. https://doi.org./10.1016/j.jpsychires.2015.07.026

Chapter Twelve: Another Mouth to Feed

1985

I'm so glad I decided to stop holding onto my friends' weed stashes because my friend Darwin had just left my house after coming from the valley when he got arrested at the base gates. He went to jail and did his time, and once he got out in the fall he came knocking at my door for a place to stay. I told him he could stay for a while, but I was on housing assistance and did not want to lose my voucher. I had two children who were more important.

A couple of days went by and one day Darwin got out of the shower, opened the bathroom door, and stood there with a towel wrapped around his waist. *All I see is this 5'9" milk chocolate man standing there with a six-pack going on and this white towel wrapped around his waist. Wow. I just can't get those pictures of him out of my head.* He never tried to do anything but my mind was racing and plotting, if you know what I mean. Within the next couple of weeks we became an item. People were surprised we were together but life happens, that's for sure.

Darwin helped with Shawn and Bradford quite a bit, especially with Shawn because he was the oldest. He showed them things like drawing, biking, cooking, and ironing because I sure didn't like ironing.

Since he was no longer in the service Darwin had to find work. He was determined so he was up every morning to look for work, and eventually he got a job. Soon he was back on his feet.

We had been going at it like rabbits, but I couldn't use birth control pills because they gave me migraine headaches. I used to get them so bad after Shawn was born my mother would have to keep him overnight. At this point I used whatever I could get my hands on, like the Today Sponge which was marketed in the 80s. Unfortunately, I found it was ineffective because I began to suspect I was pregnant again in January. *I'm pregnant again with child number three. Oh boy, another mouth to feed in my family I'm already struggling to feed.*

Soon I went to the doctor so he could confirm my pregnancy. I had brought Shawn with me, and all kinds of emotions were going through my body on my way home on the bus. When we got off the bus Shawn ran into the house. I thought he was just running to run but he ran till he was inside the house. Shawn told Darwin the news before I had a chance to fully understand I was getting ready to go through nine months of carrying a child again.

I got in the house and Darwin asked, "Are you?"

I said, "Yes." He smiled and congratulated me. *Yeah, but two other men haven't been there to support me. Why did I allow this to happen again?*

The worst part of me being pregnant again was telling my mom because she had already said, "Nobody is going to marry you with all these children." *I'm prepared for the worst but I need to let her know. She is always consoling me about something.*

With the new addition coming in September, we needed more space so we moved into a duplex apartment. Once we got the much-needed larger apartment unpacked, I enjoyed having newer appliances and a big backyard for my kids to play in. We were closer to a grocery store and the bus line was right there on the corner.

On September 1, 1986, not long after Darwin picked me up and placed me on a tree limb that was within arm's reach for him, my water broke and I was going into labor. We called a cab to get to the hospital because my baby was coming quickly. We got to the hospital and within the hour my beautiful little girl Tanesha was born. Darwin had stepped outside to take a phone call so he didn't get to experience the birth of his first child.

My blood pressure was up so I couldn't see my baby for 24 hours. I was feeling depressed and helpless because I couldn't have visitors until my blood pressure went down. Eventually my blood pressure improved and we were able to go home.

A few months passed by and God showed me in a dream that things weren't going well between me and Darwin. What I didn't realize was he had already moved on physically, but soon he proved my dream right. I already had enough on my plate without his baggage, so I sent him on his way.

We still kept in contact with each other because we had a child together, but of course, I was upset about the relationship ending and went into a deep depression. I don't think I knew I was depressed because I had learned how to cover it up. I began to drink alcohol and smoke cigarettes more heavily.

I could not have made it by myself if my brother Robertus was not there. He moved in with me to help watch the children, and I always felt safe with him there, especially when nighttime came. Shawn was also a big help because from helping out with his brother he knew how to cook basic food, do Tanesha's hair, and change diapers.

We frequently had company stopping by because I was always cooking or had the grill going. My house was the party house and sometimes there were more children visible than I could count. In spite of what seemed like good times, I became more depressed but masked it pretty well. I was always smiling and appeared to be happy when deep down inside I was feeling used and abused.

Did you know?

Smoking cigarettes and abusing alcohol are two of the foremost preventable causes of death and disability. Scientists have determined these addictive behaviors are prompted and maintained through a complex interplay of genetic, psychological, and environmental factors. When it comes to girls, traumatic experiences have been proven to contribute to the early initiation of smoking and drinking,[1] often used as a coping mechanism to avoid anxiety and depression.[2] In fact, the higher the number of adverse childhood events (ACEs), the greater the risk of nicotine and alcohol dependence in adults. Recent studies have demonstrated that smokers who were sexually abused in childhood smoke more frequently than smokers who were not abused.[1]

---

1   Cheng, S., Wen, Y., Liu, L., Cheng, B., Liang, J. Y., Chu, X., Yao, Y., Jia, Y., Kafle, O. P., & Zhang, F. (2021). Traumatic events during childhood and its risks to substance use in adulthood: An observational and genome-wide by environment interaction study in UK Biobank. *Translational Psychiatry, 11,* #431. https://doi.org/10.1038/s41398-021-01557-7

2   Hogarth, L., Martin, L., & Seedatb, S. (2019). Relationship between childhood abuse and substance misuse problems is mediated by substance use coping motives, in school attending South African adolescents. *Drug and Alcohol Dependency, 194,* 69-74.
https://doi.org/10.1016/j.drugalcdep.2018.10.009

Chapter Thirteen: Finding Trouble

1987

Within a couple of months I encountered more friends looking to buy marijuana. Even though I didn't use the product, I always knew who was selling it. This particular time I had someone looking to buy so I used my connection to help. I did this for several weeks and got money in the process, which I needed.

Things changed one night when someone wanted to buy cocaine. I called my source and let them know what I needed, and they brought it right over. The person who delivered also brought me a small care package for my service. I was introduced to a new product which was cocaine.

I still remember being in my bedroom at the back of the house, taking a little of the white powder, and putting it on the tip of my cigarette. It was the best high, but I didn't realize I was going to be hooked. People would come to buy it, and every time I sold something I was getting bigger cuts. I started smoking more of it just to ease the pain I was experiencing.

Nobody even noticed I was using this deadly drug. Before long I was hooked on cocaine and couldn't stop because I kept looking for the same high. I enjoyed how it made me feel numb to life. But I wasn't just using—I started selling coke, too.

Every day from four to six o'clock, I started going to happy hour. My brother didn't mind because I always cooked dinner ahead of time before leaving. I made sure my children were taken care of.

On a Friday night at the China Gate Club, I met another guy from the military named Thaddeus. He arrived late and was sitting all alone at a table next to mine. He was probably 5'6", dark-skinned, with a short haircut, well-groomed and seemed rather pleasant. I asked him if he wanted to dance and he said, "I really don't dance," yet he complied. I have a way of getting people to come out of their safe zone.

We ended up dancing the last few songs before they closed and then I sat at his table so we could introduce ourselves. As we were walking out of the club Thaddeus asked, "Do you want to get a burger or something?"

I said, "Yes," so he took me to Burger King. Afterward, he brought me home and we exchanged phone numbers.

On Monday, I got home from work and I had a surprise waiting for me in my bedroom. It was the most beautiful dozen yellow roses I had ever gotten and the only ones I'd ever received from a guy. The fresh smell of roses in my bedroom was exciting to me.

One evening after work, I met my good friend Martha, who was also my boss, for drinks on East Third. My new friend Thaddeus came to meet Martha. I was sitting there with my favorite drink, a Long Island iced tea, when, much to my surprise he asked me to marry him. *What? How can this be? Mom said no one would marry me with three kids. He can't be serious.* A laugh was all the answer I could give.

He started coming over with his six-year-old daughter Yolanda and we blended right away. She had a good time playing with my kids and mine didn't mind her. We would take the kids to the movies and out for dinner and everything was going well.

When I was a teenager, I had prayed I would get married at the age of 28 and adopt a child, so it seemed my prayers were being answered. I couldn't believe it was real, but he persisted until I started thinking about getting married and planning a wedding.

We dated for quite some time, but I didn't let him know about my secret cocaine addiction. I didn't want him to have any trouble with his employer due to my drug habit, and this made me realize I should put some distance between us. Soon, I was avoiding him and I stayed away for a whole year.

❧ ❧ ❧

Some months later, I was still dealing drugs; a new customer came by, and I had to find a dealer who could supply what he was seeking. At first, I used another friend as a go-between to exchange money for the package of drugs. As was my arrangement, I got my little stash as well, but after a few times of me sending someone else to pick up the product, the big drug dealer wanted to meet. I went to the hotel where he was staying and knocked on the room door.

The dealer who opened the door was named Benjamin. He was dark-skinned, had curly hair, was about 5'9" and had the most beautiful smile. The smoky room smelled like cocaine and stale cigarettes, and it was very small. I sat there on the side of the bed next to him while Benjamin prepared a rock he pulled from a jar.

"Do you smoke?" he asked. He showed me his pipe.

"Not like that," I said. "Only on my cigarette."

When he finished his preparations, he took the white rock out of the jar and put it on the pipe. He passed it to me after he lit it, and at first I said, "No," but eventually I relented and hit the pipe. *Wow. That first hit is taking me to places in my mind I never expected. I feel numb and calm for the first time since I can remember. I can hear Benjamin talking to me but I'm too relaxed to respond.*

He said, "You're high." He flashed me a beautiful smile.

"Yes." My spirit was coming alive, and at the same time I was beginning to feel paranoid because people were knocking on the door wanting to purchase Benjamin's product. *I'm not sure I feel comfortable in this new environment. Maybe it's time to go.* I gathered up what I came for but before I could go, Benjamin asked for my phone number. We exchanged numbers and then I left. As soon as I had delivered the package to my customer, I went straight back to my apartment to smoke what I had gotten from Benjamin.

❧ ❧ ❧

When my lease was up at my duplex they went up on the rent, so I had to find something that fit my income. I found a big, two-story peach-colored house in Brown's Addition. The upstairs had two bedrooms and the master bedroom was downstairs; there were two bathrooms, a fireplace, and a big backyard. The house wasn't far from the school for my two boys. The landlord and I set up for a housing inspection and it was approved, so we were able to settle into our new home.

Meanwhile, I continued going to see Benjamin in his hotel room. Although I was there to pick up purchases for people, one thing led to another and we became lovers. I began spending more time with Benjamin during the evenings while my babysitter Cindy watched the kids. By this point I was hooked on the crack pipe and was starting to do more each day.

Soon Benjamin got put out of the hotel he was living in and moved in with me. Now I had people I didn't know constantly at my door.

One day, someone knocked and I went to the front door with my daughter in my arms and opened it up. I saw a whole SWAT team on the front lawn, and a heavily armed man in uniform was flashing a badge at me. The police ran in, searching everywhere, while I sat on the floor behind the couch with a policeman standing guard over me. *What's going to happen? I've never been involved with the police before. This is horrifying.*

The officer who was guarding me said, "We arrested Benjamin a couple of blocks from your house," but whatever they were looking for, it wasn't there. After they finished searching the house and asked me a few more questions, they all got in their patrol cars and left.

I don't want to go to jail or lose my kids for something I brought on myself. Boy-oh-boy, how did I allow this to happen to me? Is it greed for the white powder? Am I hooked or just naive? Whatever the case, I didn't see this coming. I'll never do dirt where I lay my head again.

❦ ❦ ❦

The week before the police came, Mom had come to visit me and the kids. She prayed through the house that morning, and I felt the presence of God when she left. Mom was always on her knees praying, and when we were younger, we kneeled around the bed with her.

The raid seemed like the worst thing that could happen to me, but it changed me for the better because I decided to give my life to the one person who protected me all these years from birth till now and saved me from going to jail. God is His name and on February 19, 1988, I went to church and gave my life to Christ. *Dear God,* I prayed, *I promise I won't ever use again if You will deliver me from that dark world of being paranoid, restless, with no appetite, and losing weight.*

It was time to say enough is enough. I had to make a choice for the betterment of myself and my family. I chose my three kids over the white rock and today I am ever thankful I've been free from that powdery substance for 35 years. I quit using crack cold turkey and had no withdrawals or cravings because God delivered me from it. I reconnected with Thaddeus, and by September I married him and embraced his daughter Yolanda as my own, just like I had dreamed of for so many years.

Did you know?

Childhood sexual abuse not only makes adult survivors more likely to smoke cigarettes and abuse alcohol but also to abuse illegal substances such as cocaine.[1,2] This population tends to abuse substances to boost their self-esteem, deal with isolation and loneliness, handle or suppress bad memories, and cope with symptoms of anxiety and depression.[2] As if addiction weren't enough, the National Institute of Justice reports survivors of childhood sexual abuse are at risk for criminal behavior such as drug-related offenses, property crimes, and prostitution. While most are never arrested, the risk of criminal activity is higher for survivors of childhood sexual abuse than for people who did not experience maltreatment in childhood.[3]

---

1   Tonmyr, L., & Shields, M. (2017). Childhood sexual abuse and substance abuse: A gender paradox? *Child Abuse & Neglect, 63* (Jan. 2017), 284-294. https://doi.org/10.1016/j.chiabu.2016.11.004

2   Lohmann, R. C. (2018, Jan. 26). Childhood sexual trauma and addiction: Understanding child sexual abuse and drug use. *Psychology Today.* https://www.psychologytoday.com

3   National Institute of Justice. (1995, March). *Victims of childhood sexual abuse– Later criminal consequences.* US Department of Justice. Office of Justice Programs. https://www.ojp.gov

Chapter Fourteen: Are You My Mother?

1989

Growing up, I was told I had long fingers like my dad who raised me. After I learned I was adopted, I knew that wasn't true. I had birth parents with my DNA who existed out there somewhere.

I was always searching for my parents, especially when we would go to the mall on Saturdays. I was looking for someone my color, which is dark brown, with long black hair, black eyes, and wearing glasses. I was so obsessed with the book *Are You My Mother?* by P.D. Eastman that I could recite it.

In 1988, I had put paperwork in to look for my birth parents and whoever else might be my blood relatives. To my surprise, the following year I located my parents and seven of my siblings.

When I flew over to Tacoma, Washington to meet my birth mother, she came along with a couple of her friends for support. I stood by myself waiting to meet her, feeling alone like I did when I was told I was adopted at the age of five or six. Finally, I saw three smiling ladies approaching me in the airport for an embrace. I'll never forget when my birth mother said, "I'm your mom." It was rather awkward since I already had a mom.

I couldn't call her "Mom," so I just said, "Hello."

That night I stayed at my birth mother's house and I will never forget when I saw her in the morning; we had on the same red, black, and white colors. We went out to breakfast and ordered the same breakfast from Waffle House. I love over-easy eggs, hashbrowns with sauteed onions, and pancakes. Not only did we have similar tastes, but I was pretty excited to look at her and see all the features I had in common with her. My long hair and fingers made sense when I saw hers.

I got to spend a little time with my birth mother before I went overseas to the Philippines when Thaddeus got stationed there. Once we were in the Philippines, we kept in contact with each other through letters. My birth mom, Barbara, would even send her delicious zucchini bread over to us. I would pick it up at the post office on base and we would open it and begin eating before we got home.

I returned to the states before Thaddeus, and as I was waiting for him to come home from the Phillipines I moved to Airway Heights, a town near Spokane. One Sunday when I got out of church and was heading home, I stopped at a light on East Second. I noticed a car to my left and looked over to see a familiar-looking man. We glanced at each other, the light changed, and we drove off, but I didn't know until later he was related to me. When I finally met my brother Tobias face-to-face, we both said, "Hey, I saw you at the light on East Second."

It was like we had known each other forever with never a dull conversation. The connection I felt that day with my youngest brother was something I was missing all those years before I met my birth mother and family. The pieces of my puzzle were slowly starting to connect.

I heard from my three sisters and one brother. We all started corresponding with each other through letter writing. Our lives were beginning to sound identical as we had all gone through something. We were all angry because for so long we didn't know whether our parents were dead or alive. I was so excited to have such a large family; I just thanked God for allowing me to meet them all except for one sibling. We had all survived except for my brother James who was the oldest and was killed in

California before I had the chance to meet him. From what my brother Trevor said, he was always into something to keep busy. If I didn't know any better, I'd think he was on a mission to accomplish things before his life was to be cut short.

It was amazing that I could finally identify with someone like me. When we gathered together, the chitter-chatter in one room with all of us was like a train at full speed. We all talked fast and were able to understand each other. In the past with my adoptive family, I would have to repeat myself several times for people to know what I was saying. My new family all ate fast like it was going to be our last meal. "Slow it down a bit," I was told growing up, but wasn't quite comfortable with that. I had finally met my match—we just ate and didn't care how fast or how slow.

Something else I noticed about us is we all liked to work and were quite successful. Our parents, even though we had different adoptive and foster parents, must have instilled in us the desire to take care of ourselves and to build an empire if we wanted. My adoptive mother wanted us to have the best etiquette, clothes, schools, vocabulary, etc. for her kids. My adoptive Dad, on the other hand, made sure we understood about cars and gardening, and taught us not to be so loud out in public along with other things. As I am writing this I finally figured out why I am so quiet when I am out in public.

The more we got together as a family the more I was able to connect the puzzle pieces. We were a family that never separated in spirit. What a blessing to have my siblings touch and give me hugs; that meant the world to me. Looking at our postures we were all identical in some way or fashion. My sisters always laughed at me because I was the only one with a big butt at the time. I made fun of them because they had the big breasts I always wanted. Every time we got the opportunity, we were either talking on the phone or writing until we could meet in person. What an awesome blessing to be able to reconnect with my birth family after being placed in the care of others.

In my travels I have come in contact with several people who were adopted and were curious about my outcome. I shared the good and the bad. After speaking with them and sharing my experiences with my birth mother and siblings I would tell them how and where to start their search. I would also tell them to write down why they wanted to search. I searched because I was having heart problems and wanted to know the family history. When I would go to a doctor the first question they wanted to ask was about my family medical history. I got tired of saying, "I'm adopted," and "I don't know." It was my right to know who my biological parents were.

I often find men are more apprehensive about finding their biological parents. Most say they don't want to get hurt again or they just don't want to know. I have honored what they say but still let them know someone could be out there who may be looking for them.

I let them know getting connection with my bloodline is one of the most beautiful gifts I have ever gotten. Not only will their children become a part of a new family, but they will also be able to connect with cousins who have similarities.

Did you know?

When adopted people and their birth relatives choose to search for one another, they need all the resources they can get. The Child Welfare Information Gateway is a great starting point for a wide range of helpful resources, such as information on state laws, adoption registries, DNA testing, and best practices.[1]

---

1   Child Welfare Information Gateway. (n.d.). *Searching for birth relatives.* Children's Bureau: Administration for Children and Families: U.S. Department of Health and Human Services. https://www.childwelfare.gov

Chapter Fifteen: Do I Have a Sign on My Forehead?

2015

After finding my birth mother and siblings in 1989, the subsequent years brought many changes, including a move across the country to Jacksonville, Florida and a divorce from Thaddeus.

Sherri with her fiancé, Cleveland.

One day, I decided to go on a walk by myself. Usually, my fiancé and I would walk together, but not this day in May. During my beautiful morning walk back home around 9:30 a.m. on a sunny day on Harts Road here in Jacksonville, I saw a guy who was standing on the opposite corner by a stop sign with his eyes fixed on me.

While I was enjoying my walk home, I noticed he kept his eyes on me the whole time. I had no clue what was going to happen next. As I got closer to him, he started crossing the street coming into my path.

We met and he spoke in a rather soft voice while I just nodded my head and kept it moving. I slowed down my pace so he could pass ahead of me, but he didn't.

A lady on her green bike was standing on the opposite side of the street. The man yelled to her, "What time is it?"

At that point I was able to get a sense of what clothes he had on: brown, dirty, khaki pants, a dingy white t-shirt, and a pair of rundown, soiled tennis shoes with no socks on. His black hair looked filthy and nappy like he wasn't taking good care of himself. As we continued walking over a bridge, I assumed he would go on about his business.

I picked up my pace and started walking faster. I had my keys in my pocket so I placed them between my fingers, keeping my hands in my pockets. When I looked back he was still close behind, and I should have crossed the street but didn't. I had a strange feeling in my gut; all I knew was I should get home to safety. As I was passing the church on the opposite side of the street, I heard God say, "Don't be afraid." At the same time the stranger grabbed me from behind so tightly I couldn't move; all I knew was I had a voice and I used it that day to the max. Cars were going up and down Harts Road but no one stopped to help.

The man eventually let me go, and as he ran across the street, he almost got hit by two cars. I was frantic, so scared I couldn't even dial 911 or my fiancé.

A man and his son who were headed to softball practice pulled over on the opposite side of the street and called 911. The man walked over, asked if I was okay, and said the police were on their way. Then he called my fiancé so I could tell him what happened.

The police came and swarmed the area asking me all kinds of questions. Thanks to the gentleman who called the police, they had captured the dirty young man about 10 blocks from where he grabbed me.

I had to ride around the corner in a police car to identify the guy and as soon as we pulled up, I cringed with fear. "Yes, that is him," I said, and they arrested him.

I felt lucky he was captured because he could have taken me into the woods right there and no telling what could have happened. It was broad daylight, and I never thought anything would happen to me like this. Eventually, we went to court only to learn he was found incompetent to stand trial. He had a mental illness and they couldn't hold him for a long period.

Everything I had suppressed came back up to haunt me, even though it was 38 years after I was first sexually assaulted. I was afraid to go anywhere by myself because the trauma of that day was always present. The same questions came up again—*what did I do to deserve this? Why? Do I have a sign on my forehead?*

Did you know?

In the aftermath of childhood sexual abuse, the victim may experience symptoms of post-traumatic stress disorder (PTSD), such as flashbacks, sleep disturbances, hypervigilance, intrusive thoughts, and changes in memory, as well as anxiety and depression. The trauma of abuse results in changes to the brain which may last long after other symptoms have subsided.[1] As a result, when people encounter new situations that remind them of the environment or dynamics of their previous traumatic incident, they may become retraumatized; in other words, they reexperience the distressing symptoms of PTSD. The article referenced below provides helpful suggestions about self-care for victims who have been retraumatized.[2]

---

1   Sherin, J. E., & Nemeroff, C. B. (2011). Post-traumatic stress disorder: The neurobiological impact of psychological trauma. *Dialogues in Clinical Neuroscience, 13* (3), 263–278. https://doi.org/10.31887/DCNS.2011.13.2/jsherin

2   Sullivan, S. (2017, Oct. 6). *7 ways survivors of sexual violence can practice self-care when retraumatized during tragedy.* National Sexual Violence Resource Center. https://www.nsvrc.org

Chapter Sixteen: My Healing Journey

Healing was not something that happened in one magical moment. It was a process, a journey that began even as my story was still unfolding. Many nights I cried, wishing I had spoken up and said something. Fear takes you to places you don't want to be. What I know now and want to share with anyone reading my book is to pay close attention to your children. I was a book no one read. It wasn't till I was 27 years old when I told my mother after visiting her one afternoon in 1986.

Mom was sitting on the couch watching Opera Winfrey. Oprah was sharing her story about her abuse at the hands of her cousin. I began to cry and told Mom about Stan. My mom cradled me in her arms until my tears stopped. Then she asked, "Why didn't you say anything?"

"Because I was 14. He threatened me and the whole family if I said a word about it to anyone."

Mom began to weep. "I'm so sorry," she said. *For the first time in 14 years, I feel so relieved.*

When I was attacked again in 2015, I went to all of the perpetrator's court dates to no avail, and they just kept pushing the trial date back. It was as though they knew there was nothing they could do because eventually, the man was found incompetent to stand trial. To this day I am still angry about our mental health laws when it comes to rape and assault victims.

As awful as the experience was, my grandchildren were there to support me, and it allowed me to educate them about the seriousness of rape. I shared my own story with them so they would learn the importance of getting help, both to stop the perpetrator and to heal themselves.

My grandchildren learned they have the right to set healthy boundaries, even with people they know. "You don't have to let anyone touch you without your consent," I explained, "not even a relative. If anyone ever crosses the line with you, I hope you feel empowered to report it because it's not your fault and you deserve support. Don't listen when the perpetrator threatens to harm you because *no* means **no**."

I had made a promise to myself that one day I would do something to help other women, so after the disappointment of learning my attacker would not stand trial, I recovered my sense of power by starting a non-profit organization called Women United Against Sexual Molestation (WUASM) in 2015. During the process of sharing my story, I began to heal as I leaned on my faith. We prayed the Serenity Prayer used in 12-step programs, and we worked from the book *Lord, Heal My Hurts* by Kay Arthur.

What a relief to know you're not the only one. Little by little, I was able to pour out my soul to other women and men with like stories. I was able to share my story in detail, everything that happened, leaving out nothing. After years of keeping the frightened little girl boxed and locked inside, I was able to touch them to help them open up and want to share their story. I was able to cry and give them the hugs we should have received when sexual abuse changed our lives. I was finally able to start finding out who Sherri is just from listening to their stories.

Sherri representing WUASM at the Jacksonville Women's Expo.

After everything I have been through, I have learned some choices I made in life were bad choices on my part. Like getting on the back of my brother's bike and falling off and spraining my right wrist. That was a choice when I was told not to get on the bike. And I should have still been home until I graduated from high school, but that was another choice.

When I was raped and carried the pain for 14 years until I told my mom, I didn't have forgiveness for either perpetrator. I harbored hate in my heart. I felt abandoned by my birth parents, abandoned by my adopted parents who had no idea what had happened to me. I left home at the age of 17 because I didn't know what forgiveness truly was.

After I started my non-profit and shared my story, people always asked, "How do you forgive?" Even though I hadn't forgiven my abusers, I always gave them the scripture from Matthew 18:21-22:

> 21 Then Peter came to Jesus and asked, "Lord, how many times shall I forgive my brother or sister who sins against me? Up to seven times?"

> 22 Jesus answered, "I tell you, not seven times, but seventy-seven times."

Although I knew I still needed something more, I would quote healing scriptures like Psalm 51:10: "Create in me a clean heart, O God; and renew a right spirit within me."

My heart wouldn't let me rest with the question that kept coming up, but eventually I had to face the issue. That day came in 2020, when I was out shopping in Washington, and out of the blue, I began having a panic attack. I was shaking, hyperventilating. My heart was pounding right out of my chest.

I tried taking deep breaths to make it go away but it became stronger. I turned my car around to go back to my mom's house but then began thinking. *God has a strange way of doing things.* It was as if I had no control of my steering wheel and God took me right to my cousin Stan's house. Boy, was I shaking in my boots. *What am I doing here? Do I go in or what?*

I got out of the car, saw a neighbor outside to the right of his house, and said, "Does Stan still live there?"

The neighbor said, "Yes."

I opened the gate and proceeded to walk up the lonely sidewalk, not knowing what to expect. I knocked on the door hoping he wouldn't answer. Just when I thought no one would come to the door, I heard, "Who is it?"

"Sherri."

"Sherri … really?"

Stan was opening the door when I said, "Yes." We stood there, face to face for a moment. *Is this what shock feels like? No telling what is going through his head.*

He started talking about family down south, but I cut him off and said, "I didn't come here to talk about family. I came to tell you I remember what you did to me when I was 14 years old." Stan dropped his head. "If God can forgive me for things I have done wrong, then I forgive you for what you did to me." His head remained down as I walked off his porch, got in my car, and drove off.

I traveled around the corner and parked, then I cried like a baby. For the first time in years I felt in control of my actions. I had the upper hand because I was able to release all the hatred, pain, and anxiety I had bottled inside me. I forgave my perpetrator and was ready to soar like an eagle.

I am no longer the girl in the dusty box on the shelf, a 14-year-old girl who was stuck in the past. I am now a strong woman ready to help other women deal with the fallout of what happened to them back in the day.

🦋 🦋 🦋

Trauma can last for years and years. When Stan brought me the Lifesaver Storybook candy so long after Christmas, I don't remember if I ever ate the candy or not. Maybe one day the light will come on and I will remember what I did with that box of candy I used to like as a child. Years passed in my adult life, yet I still cringed when I saw it on the shelves every Christmas season. Until 2020, I couldn't stand to pick up a Lifesaver Storybook candy box and purchase it for my grandkids.

After meeting with my abuser, I was in the store around Christmastime and just happened to walk down the candy aisle. To my surprise, I looked up and saw the Lifesavers Storybook candy box and I froze. Like many other times, fear and difficult emotions arose in me, so I left it on the shelf. I walked quickly to get away from the aisle, but then I stopped and said to myself, "I am free from this torment of years gone by."

Once I acknowledged the feelings I had kept hidden deep within my soul, I went back and grabbed a couple boxes of my favorite candy, stood there with a wide smile, and said out loud, "It's not the candy that hurt me." I bought my candy, walked out of the store, and have been buying them ever since that day. At that point in my life, all fear was gone and I was set free.

Did you know?

To understand the importance of forgiveness, we first need to understand its opposite—anger and hostility. Anger that incites constructive action is positive, but when it has no outlet and it's allowed to fester, it becomes toxic. Toxic anger affects both mental and physical health, making people more anxious, robbing them of valuable energy, diminishing immune responses, and causing or exacerbating heart disease. On the other hand, practicing forgiveness can boost self-esteem and reduce stress levels. Forgiving requires hard work that includes coming to terms with one's pain and suffering, finding empathy for the perpetrator, forgiving, and then maintaining the feeling of forgiveness. Although anyone can practice forgiveness, religious people find prayer offers an additional measure of support. It's no accident that each of the major world religions places a high value on being forgiving, but whether or not you believe in the biblical philosophy of forgiveness, there's no denying its benefits.[1]

---

1   Weir, K. (2017, Jan.). Forgiveness can improve mental and physical health: Research shows how to get there. *American Psychological Association Monitor on Psychology, 48*(1). https://www.apa.org/monitor

Epilogue

Everywhere I go, it seems there is an opportunity to start a dialog about sexual assault. My last encounter with someone was at my doctor's office when I was talking with another patient about how I started smoking cigarettes and when I quit. Before I could finish, the woman was telling me what happened to her in her childhood. She began recounting how her stepfather was sexually molesting her and her sister while the mother knew. I can't even fathom how that feels and the emotions they carried for years. Even when the girls tried to tell other family members, no one believed them.

So many young girls and boys have been tormented by this sick behavior, left feeling ashamed and afraid to tell their loved ones. We fear no one will believe us anyway, so we just learn to cope and keep moving. Our joy is gone. No more playing games with our siblings because we can't concentrate. When we're at school our grades drop. We have low self-esteem and trust issues; our whole persona is off, but no one notices because everyone has their own issues going on. If we do respond to someone asking what is wrong with us, we automatically tell a lie and say, "Nothing."

We end up putting ourselves in a box and throwing away the old rusty key. Some women (and men) have carried pain that has been locked away for years. The old box on a shelf at a museum has never been dusted off—it sits there closed with a lock on it so it's not disturbed. But it is time to find the key and unlock what we have stored away, kept a secret for years to protect the one who hurt us as children by taking our innocence.

Who am I? Well, my name is Sherri, after being adopted by two beautiful people. Finding Sherri has been a journey since birth as you have read in my story. I believe I have finally put all the puzzle pieces together and I can now rest knowing I have finished writing my first book. Thanks again to my son and others who inspired me to write my story.

United we stand together as a group of women who have healed or may still be in the healing process. God bless you, and I urge you to help someone find the key so they can unlock their lives, get out of the box, and start their journey to healing.

About the Authors

Sherri Noble Jones lives in Jacksonville, Florida. Although she has survived many traumatic experiences including rape and is not a licensed professional counselor, Sherri brings trauma awareness to many, including women, men, and children of all ages, as well as her grandchildren.

Sherri has shared her story with her nonprofit organization Women United Against Sexual Molestation (WUASM) and others:

Channel 4 News, Jacksonville, Florida
River City Live, Jacksonville, Florida
Jacksonville Women's Expo, Jacksonville, Florida
Orlando Women's Expo, Orlando, Florida
Duval County Jail, Jacksonville, Florida
Program Success Newsletter, Daytona, Florida
First Thursday Coffee at ECCC, Spokane, Washington
Protestant Women of the Chapel (PWOC), Lakenheath, England
Black Lens News Paper, Spokane, Washington

To learn more about Women United Against Sexual Molestation (WUASM), go to wuasm.org.

To contact Sherri, email sherri.jones@wuasm.org.

Amy Cherie Copeland has been a professional writer for over 30 years. In addition to her corporate assignments, she has published a feature on Mary Miller in Jacksonville Mayor Donna Deegan's book *The Good Fight* (published as Donna Hicken); commentary, news, and features in the *Florida Times-Union*, *Jax Lookout*, and the *Miami Times*; as well as poetry in Women Writing for (a) Change's first anthology, *A River Rising*. A seasoned public speaker, she has read her poetry at the Jacksonville Women's Center's Surviving to Thriving event and performed at the Jacksonville Coming Out Monologues. Amy makes her living as a writing coach and editor in Jacksonville, Florida, where she shares a home with her husband, Charles Beyer, and their shapeshifting cat, Vila.

To contact Amy, email amycherie120@gmail.com.